CREEPY CRAWLIES

SLIMY SNAILS

Puzzle stuff

FACTS

Your NAME

EX LIBRIS

ART

Drawing stuff

BUZZ, BUZZ

Just ADD Genius with No Jiggery-Pokery

SALARIYA

© The Salariya Book Company Ltd MMXII

1 3 5 7 9 8 6 4 2

Visit our website at **www.book-house.co.uk** or go to **www.salariya.com** for **free** electronic versions of:
You Wouldn't Want to be an Egyptian Mummy!
You Wouldn't Want to be a Roman Gladiator!
You Wouldn't Want to be a Polar Explorer!
You Wouldn't Want to Sail on a 19th-Century Whaling Ship!

PAPER FROM
SUSTAINABLE
FORESTS

A CIP catalogue record for this book is available from the British Library.

Printed and bound in China.
Printed on paper from sustainable sources.

This book is sold subject to the conditions that it shall not, by way of trade or otherwise, be lent, resold, hired out, or otherwise circulated without the publisher's prior consent in any form or binding or cover other than that in which it is published and without similar condition being imposed on the subsequent purchaser.

Published in Great Britain in MMXII by
Book House, an imprint of
The Salariya Book Company Ltd
25 Marlborough Place,
Brighton BN1 1UB
www.salariya.com
www.book-house.co.uk

ISBN-13: 978-1-908177-35-3

Visit our **new** online shop at
shop.salariya.com
for great offers, gift ideas, all our new releases
and free postage and packaging.

Prof. Zacharias Zog's

Splat-A -Fact™

ART

DOODLES

DAFT STUFF

DOT-TO-DOT

PUZZLES!

STUFF

MAZES

SPOT THE DIFFERENCE

BUGS

Activity Book

by

Prof. Zacharias Zog

and

Prof. Your name

FIND ANSWERS ON PAGE 94!

ABDOMEN

THORAX

HEAD

COMPLETE THE BUGS BELOW!

Splat-a-Fact

ALL INSECTS HAVE THREE PARTS: THE HEAD, THE THORAX AND THE ABDOMEN.

4

Complete the other
half of the shield bug

Remember this bee...

And draw him on the next page!

Splat-a-Fact

BEES' COMPOUND EYES ARE MADE OF OF THOUSANDS OF TINY LENSES.

10

CAN YOU DRAW ME FROM MEMORY?

DRAW THE OTHER HALF OF THE BUTTERFLY!

FLAP FLAP

Splat-a-Fact

BUTTERFLIES CAN ONLY SEE THE COLOURS RED, GREEN AND YELLOW.

splat-a-spot

Draw the spots on the ladybirds

12

Spot the difference 1

TURN THESE STICKS INTO STICK INSECTS LIKE ME!

Splat-a-Fact

STICK INSECTS CAN SHED AND REGENERATE THEIR LIMBS TO ESCAPE ATTACKS BY PREDATORS.

16.

Bug wordsearch 1

HEAD

J	L	P	A	F	W	A	R	Z	D
T	K	R	E	R	W	I	N	G	L
E	R	O	V	D	J	S	H	S	A
H	I	B	D	Y	C	L	N	L	N
R	D	O	I	S	K	E	A	I	T
I	Q	S	T	I	N	G	E	Y	E
Z	J	C	H	T	U	S	M	K	N
A	W	I	V	F	K	H	E	C	N
S	I	S	A	E	H	E	A	D	A
J	U	C	D	I	F	T	A	J	E

WING

PROBOSCIS

STING

ANTENNAE

LEGS

Bugdoku 2

		3	4
		1	
2			3

FILL IN THE BOXES SO THAT EACH ROW, COLUMN AND 2x2 SQUARE HAS THE NUMBERS 1, 2, 3 AND 4 IN IT.

BUZZZZ

Draw bees all over the flowers

splat-a-fact

A HONEY BEE VISITS 50 TO 100 FLOWERS IN ONE TRIP.

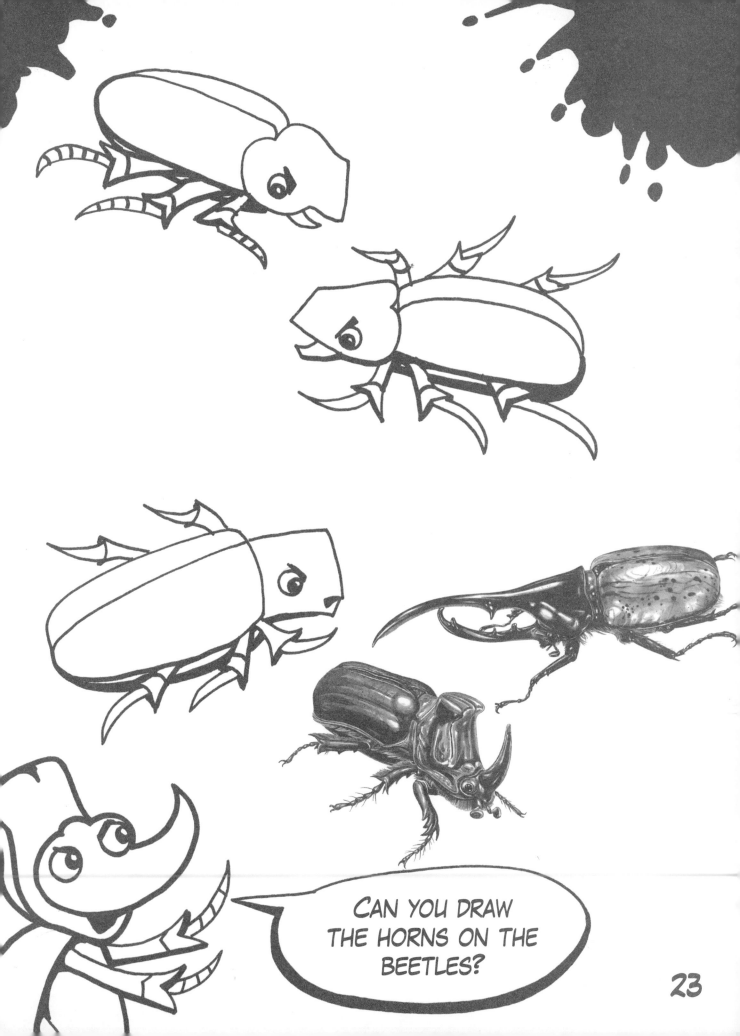

CAN YOU DRAW
THE HORNS ON THE
BEETLES?

USE ONLY THE SHAPES ABOVE TO MAKE YOUR OWN BUGS!

Create-a-Bug!

MATCH THE BUGS TO THEIR SILHOUETTES ON THE NEXT PAGE!

27

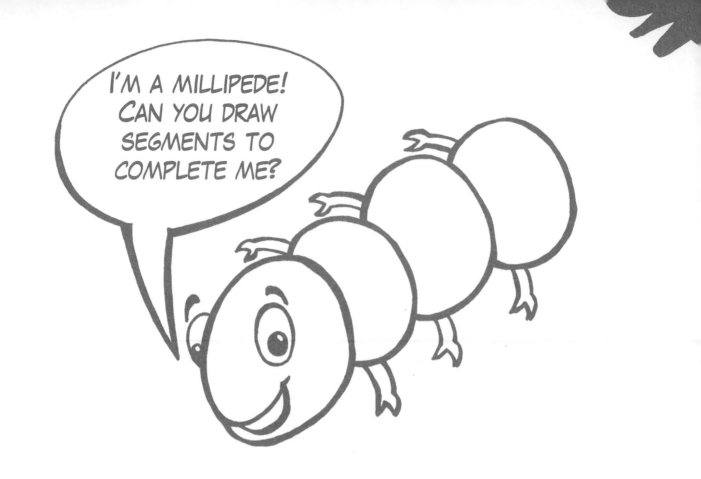

THE NUMBER OF LEGS A
MILLIPEDE HAS CAN RANGE
FROM 80 TO 400.

COUNT HOW MANY
SEGMENTS THE MILLIPEDE
HAS WHEN YOU'VE
COMPLETED IT.

EEEEK!

splat-a-fact

THE SNOW SPIDER, FROM EASTERN AFRICA, IS WHITE, BUT IT SPINS A COMPLETELY BLACK WEB.

Spot the difference 2

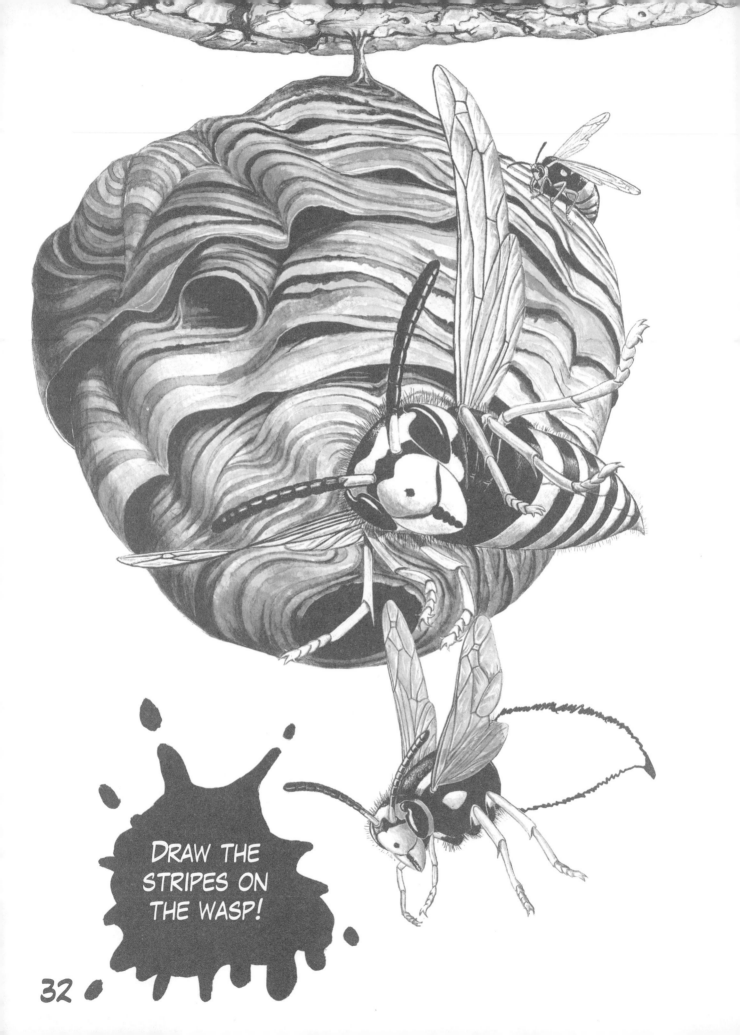

DRAW THE STRIPES ON THE WASP!

32

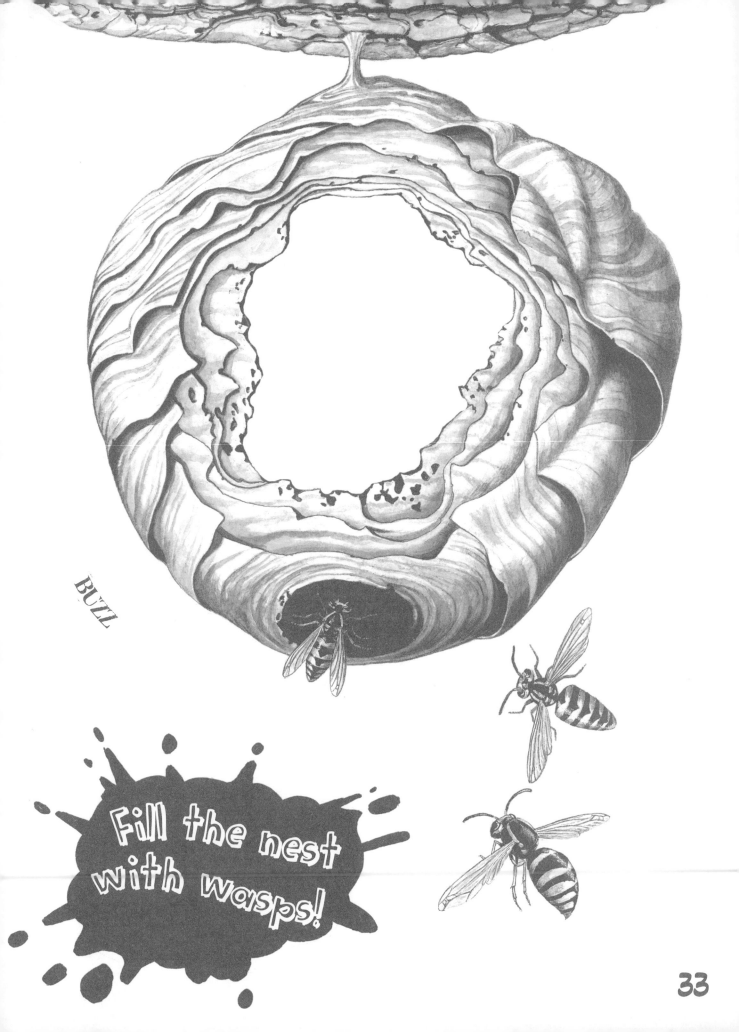

Spot the difference 3

FLUTTER

37

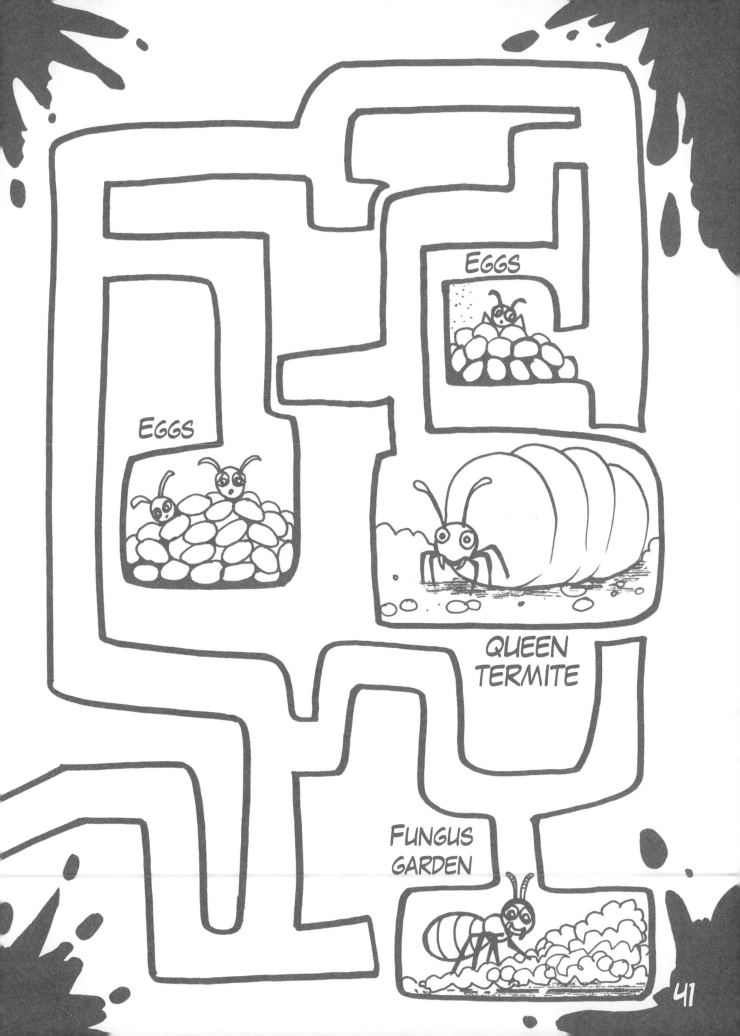

EGGS

EGGS

QUEEN TERMITE

FUNGUS GARDEN

44

splat-a-chat

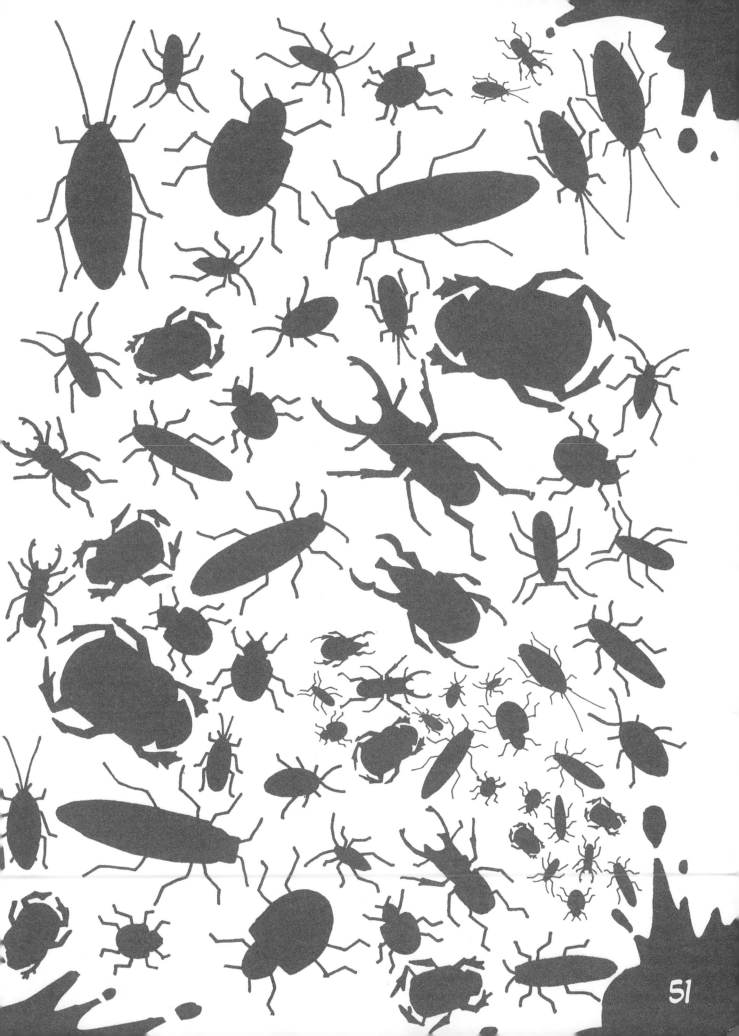

Who wins the bug battle?

You decide who wins!

WRITE THE SUPER BUGS' POWERS AND WEAPONS IN THE BOXES BELOW

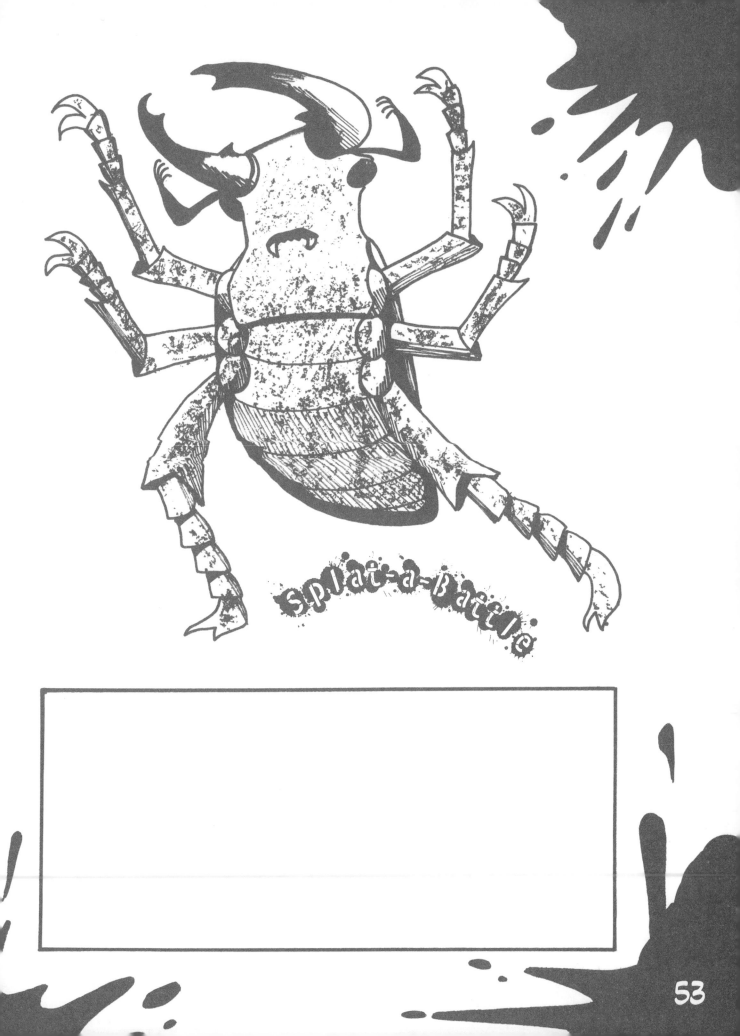

How many different bugs can you see?

54

55

56

DRAW THE
WINGS ON THE
BUTTERFLY!

58

Splat-a-Fact

THE AVERAGE LIFE
SPAN OF A
BUTTERFLY IS
ABOUT A MONTH.

splat-a-fact

CATERPILLARS TURN INTO BUTTERFLIES BY WRAPPING THEMSELVES IN A COCOON IN WHAT IS KNOWN AS THE 'PUPAL' STAGE OF ITS LIFE CYCLE.

splat-a-fact

CATERPILLARS EMERGE FROM COCOONS AS BEAUTIFUL, FULLY-FORMED BUTTERFLIES!

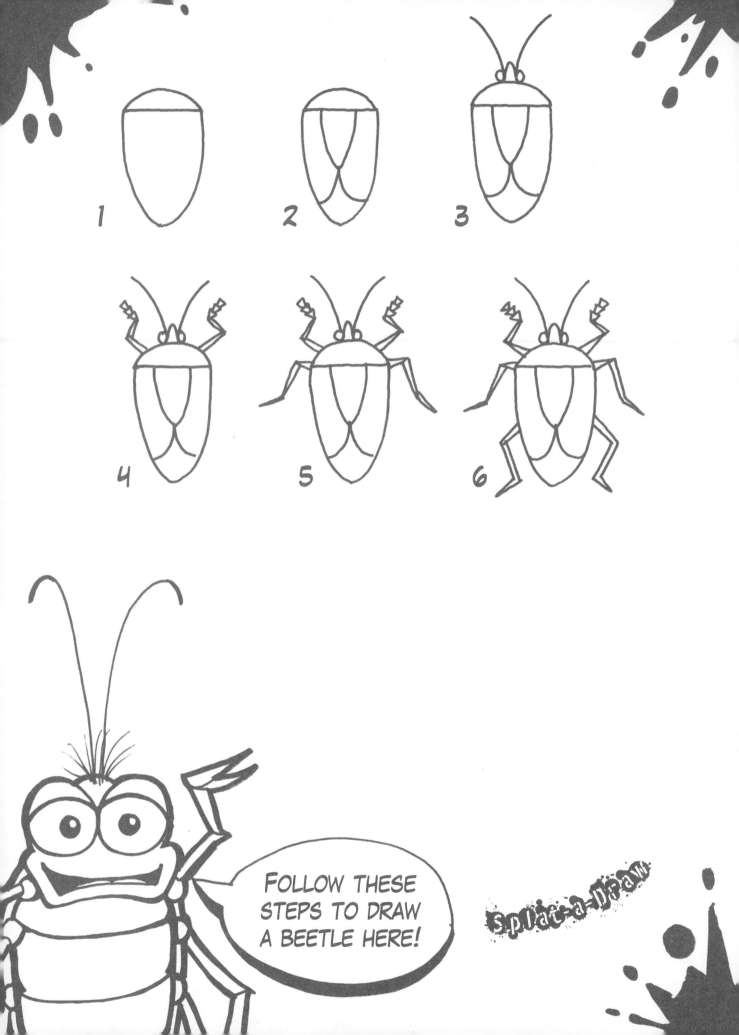

FOLLOW THESE STEPS TO DRAW A BEETLE HERE!

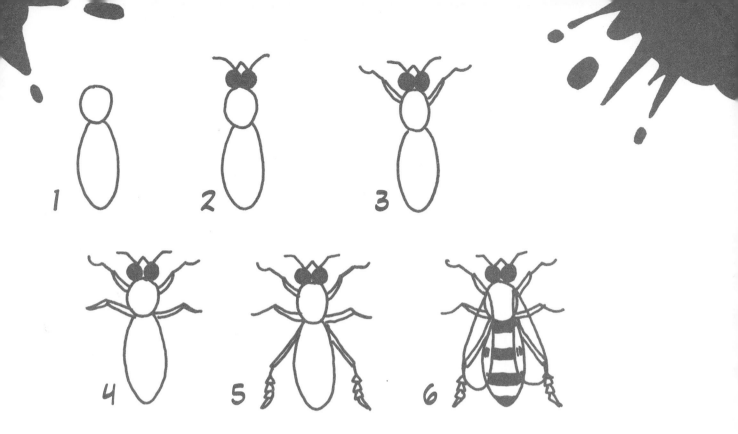

1   2   3

4   5   6

DRAW A
WASP HERE!

61

Find a way to the hive!

SCORPION

BUZZ

BEETLE

62

BIRD

SPIDER

BEEHIVE

63

Bug wordsearch 2

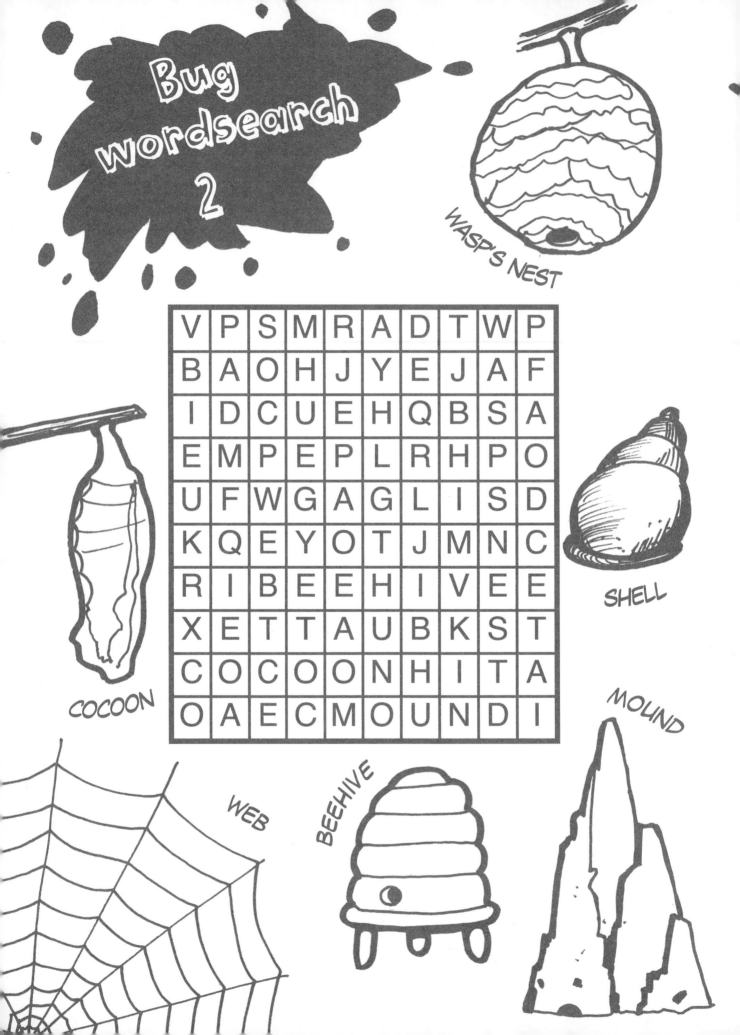

WASP'S NEST

V	P	S	M	R	A	D	T	W	P
B	A	O	H	J	Y	E	J	A	F
I	D	C	U	E	H	Q	B	S	A
E	M	P	E	P	L	R	H	P	O
U	F	W	G	A	G	L	I	S	D
K	Q	E	Y	O	T	J	M	N	C
R	I	B	E	E	H	I	V	E	E
X	E	T	T	A	U	B	K	S	T
C	O	C	O	O	N	H	I	T	A
O	A	E	C	M	O	U	N	D	I

SHELL

COCOON

MOUND

WEB

BEEHIVE

Bugdoku 3

	2		1
2			4
	3		

FILL IN THE BOXES SO THAT EACH ROW, COLUMN AND 2X2 SQUARE HAS THE NUMBERS 1, 2, 3 AND 4 IN IT.

Wow!

Draw a hand bee!

Splat-a-Fact

EACH HONEY BEE COLONY HAS ITS OWN DISTINCT SMELL SO THAT BEES BELONGING TO THAT COLONY CAN EASILY IDENTIFY IT.

69

Draw a portrait of yourself as a bug!

Splat-a-fact

THE ATLAS MOTH, ONE OF THE LARGEST SILK MOTHS, CAN BE MISTAKEN FOR A MEDIUM-SIZED BAT WHEN FLYING.

Find the 8 wasps among the bugs!

72

1

2

3

4

5

6

FOLLOW THE STEPS TO DRAW A BUTTERFLY HERE!

74

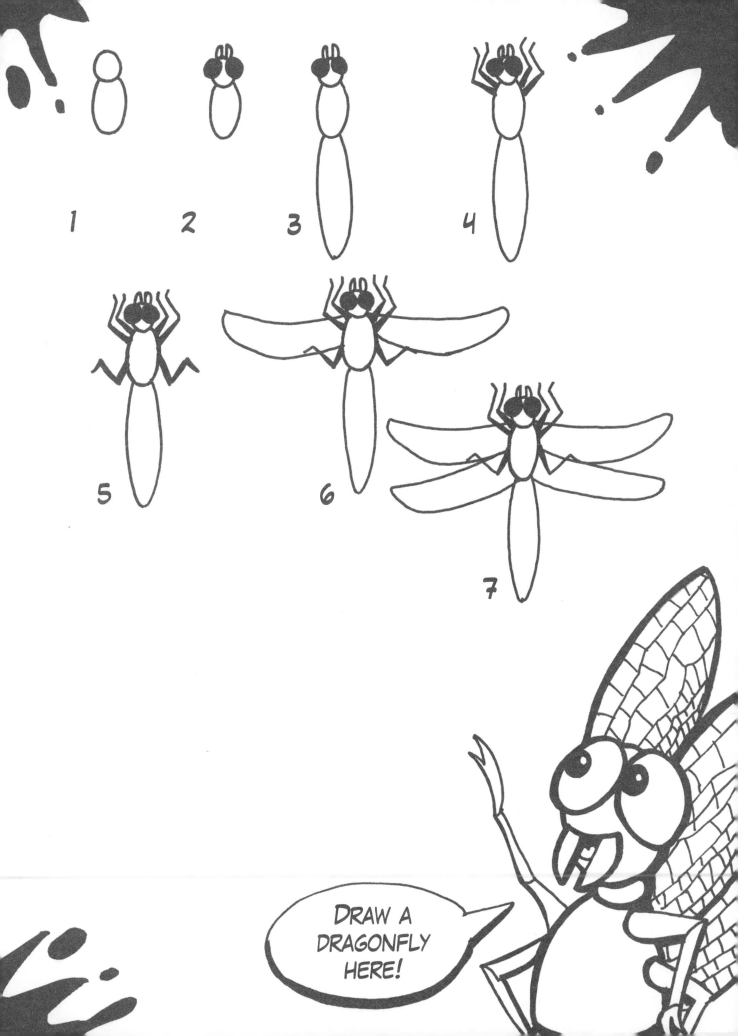

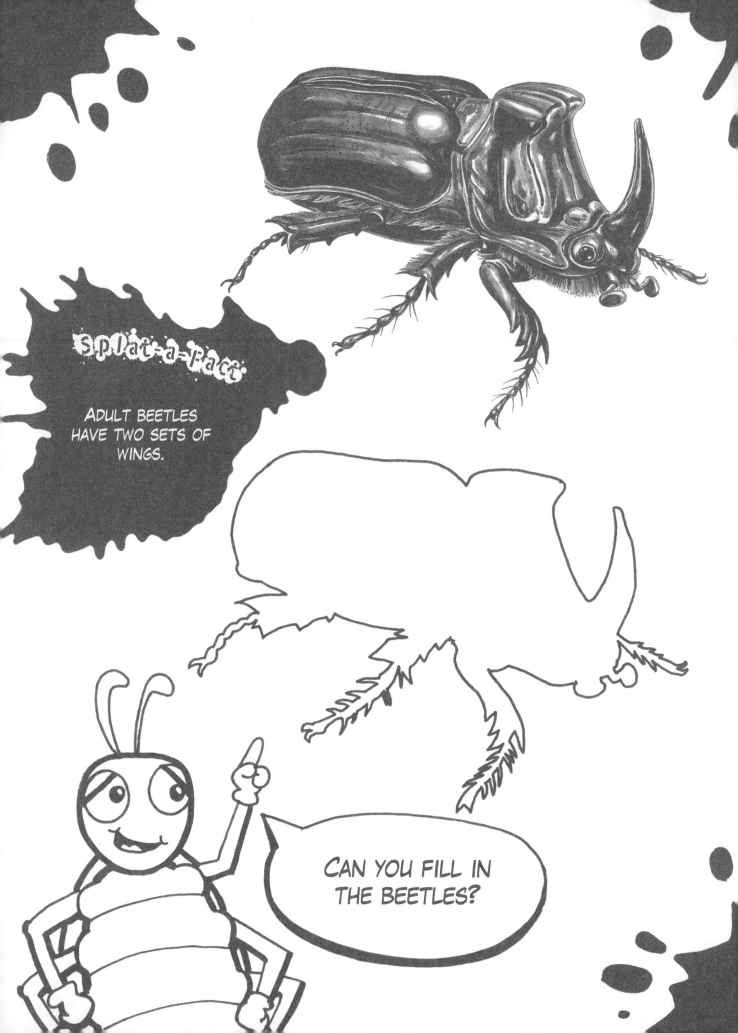

Splat-a-Fact

A PARTICULAR ASIAN MOTH HAS EVOLVED TO FEED ON THE TEARS OF BUFFALO.

BZZZT!

EEK!

Giant mecha insect!

Splat-a-Fact

THE LARGEST SPIDER EVER OBSERVED BY SCIENTISTS WAS OVER 2.4 METRES LONG AND WEIGHED 240 KILOGRAMS!

DRAW A TERRIFYING SPIDER
AND WRITE WHAT THE
EXPLORERS ARE SAYING
ABOUT IT... IF YOU DARE!

Can you find 14 dragonflies?

82

83

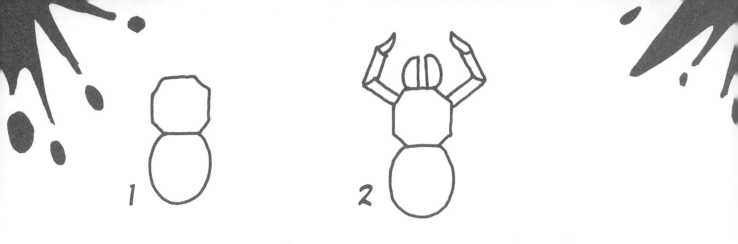

1

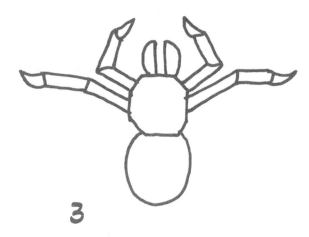

2

3

4

FOLLOW THE
STEPS TO DRAW
A SPIDER HERE!

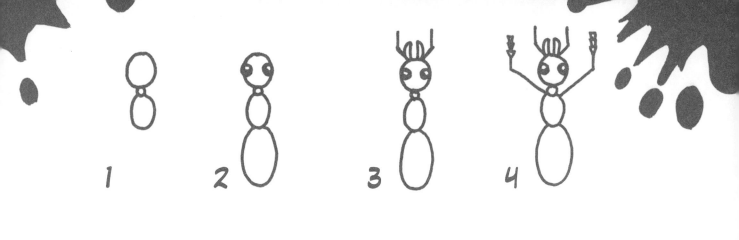

1

2

3

4

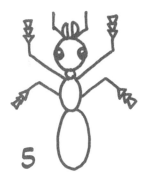

5

6

DRAW YOUR ANT HERE!

85

Colour in the butterfly wings!

90

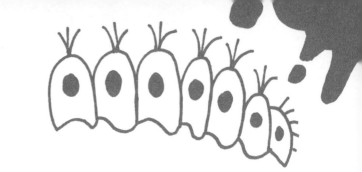

Splat-a-Fact

BUTTERFLIES AND
MOTHS ARE FOUND
EVERYWHERE ON EARTH
EXCEPT ANTARCTICA.

ANSWERS

P8: BUGDOKU 1

2	1	4	3
4	3	2	1
1	2	3	4
3	4	1	2

P14: SPOT THE DIFFERENCE 1

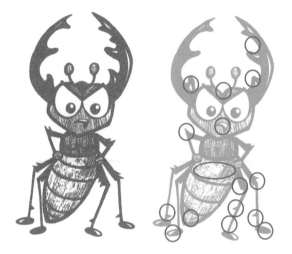

P20: WORDSEARCH 1

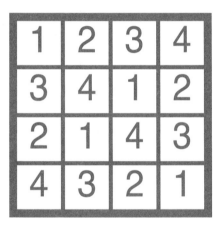

P21: BUGDOKU 2

1	2	3	4
3	4	1	2
2	1	4	3
4	3	2	1

P26: MATCH THE BUGS TO THEIR SILHOUETTES

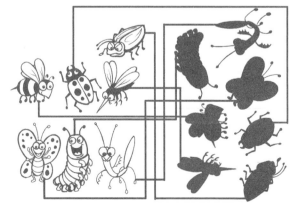

P30: SPOT THE DIFFERENCE 2

94

P34: SPOT THE DIFFERENCE 3

P40: FIND THE QUEEN TERMITE

P42: SPOT THE DIFFERENCE 4

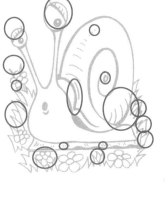

P50: FIND 14 STAG BEETLES

P54: HOW MANY BUGS CAN YOU SEE?
ANSWER: 8

P55: FEED THE LARVA

P56: CRACK THE CODE

U N D E R

B I R D B A T H

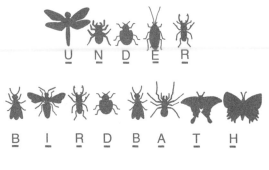

95

P64: HOW MANY BUGS ARE THERE?

ANSWER: THERE ARE 31 BUGS

P67: BUGDOKU 3

3	2	4	1
1	4	2	3
2	1	3	4
4	3	1	2

P66: WORDSEARCH 2

P72: FIND THE 8 WASPS

P82: FIND 14 DRAGONFLIES

P89: FIND 15 BEES

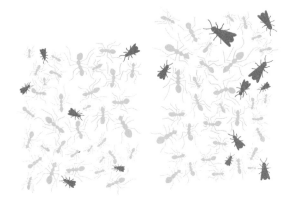